ASYLUM

DOCU-DRAMA

ERIC NGALLE CHARLES

Hafan Books

Hafan Books
c/o Tom Cheesman, COAH,
Swansea University, Wales, SA2 8PP, UK

lulu.com/hafan   t.cheesman@swansea.ac.uk

All proceeds go to
Swansea Bay Asylum Seekers Support Group

Cover image:
'The Old Man in Clyne Gardens'
carved by Nansi Hemming in 2000

Printed by Lulu.com in 2016

ISBN 9780992656492

Today I drown in my tears
while here in exile strangers
build thrones upon my
father's house. I laugh.

ASYLUM

We have seen the boat images, the dead mothers and fathers, the children dying face down in the water.

But what happens when someone makes it to the UK?

Many asylum seekers suffer from severe mental health problems. These result from the traumas that drove them to flee their home country, then their journey traumas, then their arrival traumas, then their ongoing traumas of waiting for a decision on their fate, in a strange land, in harsh poverty.

Many have contemplated suicide, many live a ghostlike existence. Many are destitute.

Indeed, to qualify for temporary Home Office accommodation and a meagre living allowance, while they wait for their case to be decided by the Home Office, asylum seekers must first prove to the Home Office that they are destitute: prove that they have no means of supporting themselves.

Strange word, destitute: from Latin 'away from having a place': forsaken, abandoned, deprived: absolutely without. Without everything. Destitution among asylum seekers means being without dignity, without having basic needs met, completely without power, able barely to survive. An animal in the forest knows it can go out and hunt, or graze, but an asylum seeker in destitution is powerless, voiceless, toothless. Without.

Constantly repeating their stories to various

agencies, they constantly relive their traumas. The stories they tell their Home Office interviewers, Home Office case workers, solicitors if they have one. The stories they tell those they meet. The stories they tell their families back home if they have any. The stories they tell themselves. It is difficult to explain trauma. How can someone retell their torture, their agony? Interviews may be conducted in front of children. A woman's tongue is tied when it comes to narrating her rape, or genital mutilation. Or a gay man or woman describing being persecuted, damned by their communities. Deep-seated aspects of their trauma are forever internalised. Some will take it to their graves.

It has taken me 16 years and I still have not finished writing my own 'last memory of my village', for all my 'integration', and all my experience working with the police, the social services, the courts, refugee community organisations.

This work focuses on a single unaccompanied male; there are far more complicated scenarios. The work is based on interviews and conversations with asylum seekers and those who've had the good fortune to move from being an asylum seeker to some kind of recognised status, such as 'refugee' or 'leave to remain'. A complete metamorphosis, you would think, but moving from one status to another is a painstakingly slow process: it brings a degree of independence; one can start rebuilding one's life again. For a while, at least. (Three years leave to remain is usually the best you can hope for.) But those who have the misfortune of not having their story believed by the Home Office, which is more often than not, rely on miniscule help from charities, and the kindness of strangers.

I thank the Welsh Refugee Council (especially Salah Mohamed) for providing facilities for creative writing workshops; Prince's Trust Cymru (especially Ebed Akotia) for supporting the workshops; Tom Cheesman for editing.

I acknowledge my debt to the ancient Welsh poem 'Claf Abercuawg' ('Afflicted, Abercuawg') –

> My spirit craves to sit a long time on a hill
> Not that I will up and go;
> My journey now is short, my home desolate ...

– and to short stories by the Sudanese psychiatrist and writer Dr Bashir Khairi: 'The Court' and 'This, or the Deluge...!', published by Hafan Books in the Refugees Writing in Wales series, respectively in #1, *Between a Mountain and a Sea* (2003, pp. 38-41) and #2, *Nobody's Perfect* (2004, pp. 58-62), both edited by Eric Ngalle Charles, Tom Cheesman and Sylvie Hoffmann.

1. IMMIGRATION INTERVIEW ROOM

Mr Marlowe

My name is Mr Marlowe, I am an investigating officer. I represent the government of the UK and HRH the Queen. I am here to interview you and determine your asylum claim. What is your name?
Client shakes his head.
Where are you from? *Client shakes head.*

Client

No understand, No understand, No understand.

Some people do understand English but develop a complex, because the authority figure in front of them comes across as threatening, giving them flashbacks.

Mr Marlowe

What is your date of birth?

Client

Shakes his head. No understand. Me No Inglis. Inglis Madrassa No.

Mr Marlowe

Hmmmmm. Most Sudanese are born on the 1st of the

1st of 1990. Do you want a cup of tea?

Client
Shakes his head, murmurs: No understand.

Mr Marlowe
Beckons his colleague: While we wait for an interpreter, can we do his finger prints? I hope this one is not from Cameroon! In Cameroon they have more than three hundred ethnic languages. Why don't they just learn English like everybody else?
Pause
Interview resumes at 2:15PM.
Small inaudible banter between Mr Marlowe and Interpreter.
I will forgive his belligerent attitude.
Are you from Syria? *(No translation.)*

Client
Me nooooo Syria. Me nooo Syria.

Interpreter
What makes you think he is Syrian?

Mr Marlowe
He looks like someone with North African appearance...

Interpreter

Do Syrians have privileges? Do they?

Mr Marlowe

How dare you make such a suggestion? Are you not familiar with *Animal Farm*? All animals are equal and all that? That is our Modus Operandi. Now moving on. What is your name?

Interpreter

Masawasmuka Arabic?

Client

Me no Arabic, Arabic Madrassa no.

A map is brought and Client identifies Eritrea.

Mr Marlowe

What is your first language?

Interview postponed. Arrangements are made with the Eritrean community to find an interpreter. Tigrinya is eventually identified as Client's first language. Meanwhile conversation goes on between Interpreter and Mr Marlowe.

So what did you make of the issue with the wristbands at Lynx House? I reckon it was all blown out of proportion, I do. You know some people compared it to the treatment of Jews in the concentration camps. Some in the Jewish community were outraged at that, they argued only one fate awaited those in concentration camp. Death. As for Mr Salah, the CEO of the Welsh Refugee Council, he said, live on television, that effectively forcing people to wear wristband equates with marking cattle for sale. I'm certain there will be backlash. I mean, when I went on holidays in Hungary, my family and I were made to wear wristbands during meal times. I support what Lynx Hotel were doing, I mean anyone could just come in from off the streets and eat from the kitchen. This country is going from bad to worse I tell you. These people come into our country, we provide them with three square meals and yet they complain about wearing wristbands. If they thought things were that bad why don't they go back to their countries? *To Client:* Do you want a cup of tea?

Client
Coffee coffee

Mr Marlowe
What is your name?

Client
Abdulkarimdawbait

Mr Marlowe

What is your name?

Client

Abdulkarimdawbait.

Mr Marlowe

How do you spell it?

Client

A for Able. B for Banana. D for Derrick. U for United Kingdom. L for Lesotho. K for Camel.,.

Mr Marlowe

Is it C for Camel or K for Kilo?

Client

K for Camel.

Mr Marlowe

Ok ok ok. Tell him for the purpose of this interview I will be referring to him as Abdul.

Do you speak any other languages? We've already established you can't speak English, I just assumed all you people speak Arabic. So you don't speak Kikuyu, Bantu, Swahili? I thought Africa as a country has many languages.

Ok Abdul, tell us what happened to you in your country. You said you were sold to Al-Qaida of Yemen, tell us what happened.

Abdul

My name is Abdul Karim Daw Bait, I was born in Eritrea on the 29th of September 1979. The last thing I remember was this question: How much fees will we be paid? A blindfold was placed over my head and I was bundled into a van.

Mr Marlowe

Do you know who these people were who placed you in the van? Did you see their faces?

Abdul

They drove for what seemed to be a very long distance, all this time I was at the back of the van bouncing and rolling around, I was tied in a fetus position. We drove for what seemed to be forever, all this time I was thinking to myself, why me, what have I done, is it because I had failed to bribe that officer who stopped me for a speeding? Was it because I had asked my manager for a pay rise, I always knew Hassan fancied my wife but even he can't destroy another man just to obtain his possessions?

Again I heard the same question, How are you paying us, they seemed to change language from Tigrinya to Arabic. I couldn't understand their accent.

The van stopped outside god knows where, I was hurriedly taken into a room and my blindfold was removed. Before my eyes could adjust to the surrounding I was slapped across the face. I had never seen so many stars before, the last time I received such a slap was when my elder brother caught me looking through the keyhole into my uncle's bedroom. My uncle's wife was at work but he'd brought home Farsana the market girl. Farsana had a reputation, but she was wonderfully beautiful and majestic in the way she walked, I could understand why my uncle was engaging in pre-marital Chichi Chorro with her, she was only twenty but she knew her way around very well. I too was developing a wantonness for Farsana, every time I saw her, I felt such protuberance.

You see in some societies Silence is Gold, Talking is Silver.

In some societies one can survive a fall from a nine-storey building, yet answering a simple yes or no question can determine life or death.

In some societies, the ruler, the King flashes his genitalia to his people.

As the slap boiled my blood, I reflected on some of

my father's proverbs. Before I could escape this reverie I was slapped again, this time I fell on the floor and banging my head. Painful as it was, the wooden floor meant I was not bleeding.

There was a fat baldy man seated in front me, his feet way too big for the sandals he wore, his toes had forced their way out of the socks like crickets who could not make up their minds if they were moving forward or retreating. I am certain his toes like myself needed some fresh air. From where I was his toes looked like something from Jurassic Park and since dinosaurs are extinct, it would have been better if the toes were kept safe in a museum in London.

The fat man looked like a government minister, he was fat not just any fat, there was no separation between his neck and his head. His belly was so big there was no way he would have been able to do his shoe laces. I thought, if I should start running there was no way he would have been able to catch up with me, let alone get out of his chair. He was surrounded by henchmen with long guns, knives and pistols, the idea of running quickly faded.

Even though the room was ridden with what looked like bullet holes and the windows were quite big, the smell was worse than that which emanates from the government mortuary across the road from the Ministry of Health.

I looked at the fat man and for a brief moment I forgot my plight, I wondered about his wife, or if he had a wife, was he gay, how he makes love, he was breathing so heavily his breath possessed the room. A punctuated whizzing followed each of his breaths, it sounded like he was dying. When my grandmother was about to take her final breath, that's exactly what this fat man sounded like.

As thoughts drifted in and out of my mind, the fat man backed some sort of orders in another language, suddenly a tiny lanky man entered the room. He looked like he'd been deprived of food for some time, his eyes blackened around the sides like one who suffered sleep deprivation. With the butt of his short gun, he hit me right in the middle of my nostril, I felt the bone crack and blood gushing, and he dragged me closer to the fat man.

I would have rather he hit me with his gun again or killed me rather than dragging me that close to the fat man. The sweat had eaten the collar of his shirt, his finger nail could be used to retrieve DNA samples in CSI. He shouted again, this time a bit of phlegm and saliva escaped his mouth and hit me directly in the face. I prayed for death, I asked for the grounds to open and swallow me, but nothing happened. I wished I had followed my father to the mosque, you see I actually do believe in God but this whole Jesus situation is making me ask more questions than answers. I tried remembering one verse in the Qur'an, all had disappeared, mysteriously.

Mr Marlowe
Interview suspended at 4pm. Would you like a cup of tea?
Alone in the interview room, Abdul contemplates.

Abdul
I am so dead, if these people do not kill me my wife will. I had promised to take our daughter to visit the Ethiopian family in Magdor Street, it would have been her first time to attend a traditional Ethiopian coffee ceremony, also, I wanted to catch a glimpse of Farsana. Farsana had captured my imagination; don't get me wrong I would always go home to my wife, but I had written two poems for Farsana and wanted to give her them personally.

'Should I throw a coin'

Should I throw a coin
into Trevi Fountain
for the legend to come true

and bring back Farsana
and she will sing again
I have heard her sing
glowingly in my uncle's bedroom
Farsana
my lover
such beautiful eyes

I have asked
why she hides behind the veil
I saw Farsana dancing
she gathers the skeleton
of her father's bee hive

Veiled
the sun red in anger
Farsana cries
her tears drift within
forming a bowl of salt
she turns into a pillar of salt

In my mind
I shouted FARSANA
she shuffled off her mortal coil
the desert wind had
separated us

Her ashes scattered
a river
with no name
her veiled face tattooed on my heart
permanently

The day before, I'd come home very late and my wife
automatically assumed I was with Mohammed. You
know you always have one friend that your wife
hates, for me that was Mohammed. If Jesus had been
married his wife would have hated Lazarus. My wife
hated Mohammed, every time he came to the house,
my wife disappeared into the kitchen doing the
dishes she'd already done.

I like Mohammed as a friend and a brother, he was
not Eritrean but Ethiopian through and through, and
he came from a family of brave soldiers. His great
grandfather fought against the Italians in the battle
of Adowa 1896. He use to entertain us with stories of
bravery, about his great grandfather and his soldier
friends, how they took advantage of the fact that they
were black and ambushed the Italians only at night.
The Italians suffered heavy casualties. Hence
Ethiopia was never a victim of colonial tentacles. He
lambasts modern warfare, he hates night vision
googles and please do not mention drone wars to
him. As part of the UN peace keeping mission in

Somalia his jeep was blown by mines left on the road side by Al-Shabaab militia men. Mohammed was well compensated, now he sits and tell us these tales of a land so far away. He always ended the battle of Adowa and the Ethiopian defeat of the Italians by saying the Ethiopians gave on up the Italians' backside, these are not his exact words.

I am certain Mohammed was the first person to own a wheelchair in the whole of our village. Pushing him on that thing was hazardous, going downhill was fine but pushing it back up the hill was a back breaker. I remember one day I was pushing him down the hill and he said, Do you know what happens to the shoes of the Moslems every time they go to pray in the mosque? As I concentrated whilst he weaved the tale, I completely forgot I was supposed to be holding his wheelchair. All I heard was Mohammed screaming as he wheezed downhill, I chased but he was going too fast. Using his military skills, he managed to fling himself out of the wheel chair into the gutter. I was terrified, when I got to him, he burst out laughing. It is safe to say, that day we didn't drink Eritrean coffee oh no, something much stronger. From Scotland. My wife would definitely kill me, if these guys do not kill me first.

Mr Marlowe

Interview resumes at 4:45. Are you sure you don't want a cup of tea?

Abdul

Tea, me, no.

Mr Marlowe

So you were dragged in front of the fat man, yes?

Abdul

Yes.

Mr Marlowe

This fat man, do you remember his name?

Abdul

No but he looked like a government minister, he looked like he was important, he was significant.

Mr Marlowe

What happened next?

Abdul

Without any warming, I was hit in the back of the head. Next time I woke up, I was in a room naked with no hand cuffs, the lanky man was standing over me zipping his trousers.

Mr Marlowe

What do you mean zipping his trousers? Were you raped?

Abdul

He left the room and brought back two buckets of water and some soap, he went out and returned with a small towel and a camera. My whole body was in pain, from my nose, my wrist my knees the back of my head my buttocks, my anal passage. The blood was dried and stuck to my skin. I slowly cleaned myself, the man in front of me took pictures. I wanted to shout for help but my voice was dead. I cleaned myself as best as I could, dried myself with the towel and applied some cocoa butter cream onto my skin. I smelled fresh.

I cried inside, silently as I remember the first time my father and I went to the Poets Garden where I first heard Mola read, that was the closest I got to my father. My father was a disciplinarian, around him we were seen not heard. He was an elder in the mosque and ensured the grip he had on the mosque was passed down to us. Loving the mosque was his first passion, his second passion was his love for camels, he had quite a few and I loved milking them. We were told consuming camel's milk guaranteed strength of muscle and character. I sincerely do not

know where we stood in his hierarchy, it was him,
his camels and his mosque. Today just my father and
I at the Poets Garden was something special, tried as
I did, our eyes never met. I remember one of Mola's
poems so very well. 'An Old Testament Eremite':

Digging holes
as we do
all this time
till the church bell rings
till the church bell tolls

I am told
I must up and go
to the hilltops and dig

The naked emperor
mourns my destiny

Holes
these are no holes

I am digging graves
for my kinsmen
and me
giving back to earth what I took
the emperor too ... ... Eremite

The lanky man gave me a white garment and red trousers to wear, really tight, I was then given a red and white scarf. I remember Yasser Arafat wearing such scarf round his head or neck. I was then brought into a room. The fat man was there, chewing what looked like tobacco, it was definitely not khat. His teeth and lips dangerously brown, he kept spitting into a pot next to him. A box was placed in front of me with blood dripping from the sides, the little soldier reached into his pockets and removed some pictures, handing them to me. He gave me another set of pictures, they were pictures of my father with his camel. I looked at the pictures in my hands then at the closed box dripping blood in front of me. I looked at the picture of my wife and daughter outside the house, such beautiful smiles, they looked more beautiful now. I looked at my father, I looked at the box in front of me, and blood was forming a small pool just by my knee. My heart started bleeding, a volcano had erupted inside me. Was today really my last day on earth? Who'd put my name in nature's calendar? Was this really it for me? I cried and begged.

Mr Marlowe
Okay, okay. What happened next?

Abdul

The lanky man bend down and opened the box, there were two heads, blood stained. My heart almost escaped my body, as it pumped faster than nature intended. Who do these heads belong to I pondered, whoever they are, they or I must have known and been very close to them, who are they I wondered out loud. The other guy kept taking pictures, all this time a camcorder was directed at me very close to me, following all my facial movements.

Do you know Yemane Ngaish? the fat man bellowed. Yemane Ngaish, do you know him?

Apparently this guy Yemane Ngaish, a Somalian journalist, had written an article which alleges that the Eritrean government had accepted huge bribes, oil and financial compensation from the Saudi Arabian government. In exchange, Saudi Arabia was going to use Eritrean military bases to launch its attack on Al-Qaida of the Yemen peninsular. This decision by Eritrea to offer support to Saudi Arabia was threatening the peaceful existence of the Horn of Africa. Ethiopia itself is really disturbed about this development. According to my abductors, I was part of the coalition working hard to bring back President Abdurabuh Mansur Hadi who was forced to flee to Saudi Arabia after Houthi rebels assaulted the capital.

My mouth was agape, I did not have a clue what these guys were talking about. My only attempt at heroics was when I ran away with some milk I did not pay for, or when I had lied to a police officer that my license was at home when indeed I have no license, I had promised to bring the officer 20 dollars the next day, but I never showed. Last I heard was that the officer had issued a fatwa on me. What were they talking about? Al-Qaida of Yemen, Houthi Rebels, President Mansur? Not a clue, not a clue.

Are you Al-Qaida? The fat man bellowed.

The little man removed another picture from his pocket collected his small knife and made a gesture like slitting his own throat.

After what seemed like an age of repeating the same question, Are You Al-Qaida? the camera was then brought much closer to me, I was handed a piece of paper in Tigrinya with this message:

"My name is Abdel Yusuf, I am a member of Al-Qaida of the Yemen peninsular, I have pledged my total support and loyalty to Al-Qaida, we will not stop until your foot soldiers have left our country. We will spill the blood of your children until you return to your country, we will chase you to the ends of the world, you infidels, first you bring the Americans here, now this."

Mr Marlowe
So did you make this pledge?

Abdul
What do you think?

Mr Marlowe
Please Mr Abdul, just answer the question. As much I am here to determine your asylum claim, I am also here to protect the citizens of the United Kingdom. If you pledged your loyalty and total support for Al-Qaida, then we might have to arrest you under the new Anti-Terrorist legislation.

Abdul
Yes I did?

Mr Marlowe
Are you now a threat to the UK? Do you represent a threat to the United Kingdom? Are you a member of Al-Qaida?

Abdul
What are you talking about?

Mr Marlowe
A simple answer Yes or No will suffice just fine.

Abdul

"My name is Abdel Yusuf, I am a member of Al-Qaida of the Yemen peninsular, I have pledged my total support and loyalty to Al-Qaida, we will not stop until your foot soldiers have left our country. We will spill the blood of your children until you return to your country, we will chase you to the ends of the world, you infidels, first you bring the Americans here, now this." They recorded my commitment over and over again and every time the word blood was mentioned, the camera moved to the box covered in blood just by my knees. Satisfied with the recording, the fat man whispered something to the lanky guy, he left the room briefly. Next thing I knew, I was hit in the back of the head. I woke up naked in the middle of nowhere no handcuffs no shoes with a sign that said, Istanbul one thousand miles.

Mr Marlowe

Is there anything you would like to add?

Abdul

Please tell my wife and my daughter that I am still alive.

Mr Marlowe

Are your wife and daughter still in Eritrea?

Abdul

So far as I know. I have not been home since that day of the kidnapping.

Mr Marlowe

For the record, would you recognize these people if you see them again?

Abdul

I can only recognize the fat man, he looked like a government official, he looked important, and he looked significant.

Mr Marlowe

Thank you Abdul, just wait for me here.

Pause.

Please sign here, sign here, sign here, sign here, sign here. Interview concludes at 6:30.

Take this letter to your solicitor, you will be hearing from us soon.

Take this letter to Migrant Help, they will help you make an application for Section 4 Support. Do you know what Section 4 Support means?

Abdul

No.

2. MIGRANT HELP, LYNX HOUSE, CARDIFF

Migrant Help was founded as a charity in 1963. Originally it was established to give support to the high number of distressed migrants arriving through the ports of Kent. Migrant Help's services have since expanded across the UK.

At the Migrant Help offices in Cardiff, a sign on the door says: "Closed from 12-2pm".

Migrant Help

Some of our workers have to attend prayers at mosque, some have their lunch; Home Office cuts mean we are short staffed. Our staff deserve a break.

Good afternoon. Have you got an appointment?

Client

No understand.

He hands over a multitude of letters and papers.

Migrant Help is packed. Men, women, children, very small room, extremely hot in the summer, cold in the winter. Little privacy. For the work they do, Migrant Help deserves a bigger space.

Migrant Help

Sit over there, let me try and find a translator.

Abdul carefully navigates through many wrinkled faces, women and children vying for help to get Section 4 support, or complaining about maltreatment by kitchen staff at the hostel next door, or trying to make an appointment to see solicitors, or trying to get money for transport to Lunar House in Croydon to make an asylum claim, or to Liverpool to submit evidence for a fresh claim.

There are people with all kinds of problems here.

One guy is not here, Rabbi. He has been identified as a troublemaker. He's been banned from all refugee community organisations. The last time he was at the Welsh Refugee Council, the police were called.

Rabbi is from Iraqi Kurdistan. About one month after converting to Christianity, his family were beheaded. He was away from his village on the day of the killings, attending a Christian madrassa. He was picked up from the school by his uncle; that was the last memory of his home. One day during creative writing sessions at the Welsh Refugee Council he was asked to write his memory of home; these are some of his poems, exactly as he wrote them:

'Three poems by Rabbi'

1

My Moda is No Home
My Fada is No Home
My Sister is No Home
My Brother is No Home
I am No Home

2

I cannot talk again
I No Voice
I No Speak
I Cry
Cry with Me

3

I don't know
How to go back Home
I can't Sleep

Migrant Help

Telephone interpreter, pay as you go rate, up to 30 minutes call plan: £65.00. Up to 60 minutes call plan: £110. Or £2.50 a minute.

Okay... I will just ask you a few questions, this won't take long.

The Section 4 support application form is at gov.uk/government/uploads/system/uploads/attach ment_data/file/261498/asylumsupportform.pdf (accessed April 2016).

On paper it is thirty-five pages long. Many questions require accompanying evidence. Most often, Section 4 support is rejected initially, because people do not have evidence to support their claim.

I need to read this to you...

Under the terms of the Immigration and Asylum Act 1999, the Secretary of State may provide, or arrange for the provision of support for asylum seekers, dependants of asylum seekers or failed asylum seekers who appear to be destitute or are likely to become destitute within a 14 day period.

An applicant is deemed destitute if:

"They and their dependants do not have adequate accommodation or any means of obtaining it, even if other essential living needs are met, or they and their dependants have adequate accommodation or the means of obtaining it, but cannot meet essential living needs."

Are you happy with that?

Tick this box: *"I have read and understood the destitution message"*

Now. Here goes.

Are you applying from within the UK: Yes / No.

What type of support are you applying for?

Section 4 Please complete sections 1 – 33.

On what date did you enter the UK? Day / Month /
Year.

On what date did you claim asylum? Day / Month /
Year.

When were you born?

Do you have a legal representative?

Assets... Have you got a bank account?

Answering yes to having a bank account means
the interview can be terminated, as you then need
to go and bring six months of bank statements. Or
the interview may continue but there's a 99%
chance your application will be rejected.

The onus (the Home Office repeats this word
often) is on the asylum applicant to prove their
destitution, in other to qualify for support.

Address...

Telephone number. Have you got a mobile phone?

Abdul

Yes.

Migrant Help

Is it a contract or pay as you go?

A contract phone means a bank account. The interview might stop or continue depending on the mood of the interviewer. Again this will constitute grounds for Section 4 support being delayed or refused for lack of proof of destitution.

OK...

Your current circumstances.

Street homeless means you will actually be sleeping on the street. Tell us when you will have no other option but to sleep on the street.

Are you or will you become destitute or street homeless within 14 days? On what day will you become street homeless? Day / Month / Year.

Who presently provides you with accommodation? Home Office / Friend / Relative / Rented.

Now...

What is your name?

How do you spell your names?

Have you got a national insurance number?

Have you got any dependants in the UK?

Do any of your dependants have any assets they can liquidate?

Cash held in the UK?

Savings accounts in the UK?
Savings held outside the UK?
Investments in the UK?
Offshore accounts?
Investments outside the UK?
Property inside the UK?
Property outside the UK?
Land in the UK?
Land outside the UK?
Valuable Jewellery?
TV/DVD/Electrical Goods?
Car/Vehicle?
Do you or any of your dependants receive any state benefits?
Have you received any support from any friends or relatives since arriving in the UK? Names / Addresses. Describe the support they provided.
Why can they no longer support you?
Tell us if there are any additional reasons why we should prioritise your application: Pregnant / Mental health problems / Serious physical health problems / Victim of domestic violence / Victim of trafficking / No additional reasons.

Hmmm. Have you got any allergies?

    Pause. Interpreter is lost, not knowing a word for allergy in their language. So too is Abdul.

Have you got any family back home?

Pause.

What religion are you?

Pause.

OK. Now the declaration.

The information you have provided in the Section 4 application form will be treated in confidence. However, it may be disclosed to other UK government departments or agencies, local authorities, law enforcement agencies, foreign governments and other bodies for immigration or research purposes to carry out their functions.

Are you happy with that?

Sign here.

Many asylum seekers are unhappy with the idea that their information may be shared with foreign governments. Also, many do not claim Section 4 support because it means agreeing to allow themselves to be deported, as well as agreeing to be relocated anywhere within the UK.

In submitting this application for support under section 4 of the Immigration and Asylum Act 1999, I understand that I am also accepting the conditions under which this support is provided. Conditions may include specific standards of behaviour, reporting, residence or complying with steps to facilitate departure from the UK.

I understand that should a decision be taken to provide me with support under section 4, it may be necessary for me to relocate to another area to access this support on a no choice basis.

OK. And finally the declaration...

I consider that I am eligible for support under Section 4 because (1) I am destitute and (2) I satisfy at least one of the following criteria:

First, *I am taking all reasonable steps to leave the UK or place myself in a position in which I am able to leave the UK. This could include complying with attempts to obtain a travel document to facilitate departure.*

And/Or *I am unable to leave the UK by reason of a physical impediment to travel or for some other medical reason.*

And/Or *I am unable to leave the UK because in the opinion of the Secretary of State there is currently no viable route of return available.*

And/Or *I have applied for judicial review of a decision in relation to my asylum claim*

And/Or *The provision of accommodation is necessary for the purpose of avoiding a breach of a person's Convention rights, within the meaning of the Human Rights Act 1998.*

Very good. Sign here. Great. Thank you. I will submit

your information now to the Section 4 team. You will be hearing from us shortly.

Go to Trinity Centre. Do you know where Trinity Centre is? Take this map, just follow it, they have all kinds of activities.

3. TRINITY CENTRE, CARDIFF

The Trinity Centre provides a safe haven for asylum seekers in Cardiff. The Welsh Refugee Council works alongside Trinity to deliver health and wellbeing meetings, play group sessions for children, leisure activities and advice. For many asylum seekers, Trinity Centre is a welcome relief. It is like the United Nations, hosting people from dozens of different countries, speaking a hundred different languages. Many volunteers here are trained in giving advice. Destitute asylum seekers go to the Trinity Centre for case appeals, Section 4 support appeals, and other legal matters. The Centre also hosts the organisation Space4U, which provides temporary accommodation and small financial support to destitute asylum seekers.
Abdul is often at Trinity Centre,

A stranger

shouts Abdul, Abdul, Abdul!
No response. The stranger walks over and pinches him. Abdul was dreaming. He realises it's his roommate.

After two days staying at the Lynx Hotel, Abdul was among the lucky ones transferred to Tanes

Hotel, off Newport Road. Tanes Hotel had its own segregation policies, but it was three-star compared to the stinking Lynx Hotel. Residents still had to go to the Lynx Hotel for meals. The procedure for meals at Lynx Hotel was like this: on entering reception, you had to sign your name on a battered green ledger which was updated once a week; once you had signed, if you had lost your wristband you had to wait and plead to the sensibilities of whoever was on reception. You would be grumbled at or chastised for losing your wristband and you would be told vehemently that failure to wear your wristband meant no food and that if such behaviour continued you would be reported to the Home Office. The Home Office was used as a byword for mental abuse and torture. Few of the people who frequent Lynx Hotel speak good English but all know the name Home Office, associated with acceptance or refusal of their cases, detention or deportation, therefore fear and dread.

Once through the reception into the kitchen, you had to sign your name again into another green ledger. Failure to sign meant the Section 4 Team would be contacted, that was the threat used by the receptionists. There was one short guy, from the Sudan I think, I'm sure he suffered from small man syndrome: he implemented this policy as if he was the Home Office himself. Draconian.

In the part of the Tanes Hotel for asylum seekers, there was no wifi, and just one small washing machine catering for everyone, which had been broken. The manager said it was broken by "an asylum". Those who spoke English challenged him and were allowed to use other machines to wash garments when the hotel was quiet. Wifi was still a no-no.

Abdul likes going into the centre of Cardiff, Queen Street, the Morgan Arcade, there's a coffee shop there, the Uncommon Ground Coffee Roastery, where the smell of the roast beans reminds him of home. This café became Abdul's hiding place until they noticed he wasn't buying any coffee. He was banned from the premises. Now he just passes and smells the air.

His case having been refused by the Home Office, Abdul is not entitled to any public assistance. The technical term is NRPF: No Recourse to Public Funds, whether for housing or food, clothing or any of life's other necessities. He is evicted from the Tanes Hotel. He is 'street homeless' and starving.

Abdul collapses inside the Trinity Centre, an
ambulance is called, he's taken to hospital.

He dreams of Sufi mystics and beautiful Arabian
women throwing flowers on his path, he sees his
wife, he sees his daughter, and he sees Farsana,
though blurred, Farsana's face, and her waist that
still gives him such a protuberance.

He remembers the last thing the Judge had said
during his father's trial: Death, Death.

Trinity Centre
Mr Abdul, take this letter to the Red Cross on Friday.
They will be at the Welsh Refugee Council. Do you
know where that is? Take this map.

The Red Cross provides weekly support of ten
pounds and clothing vouchers. Yes indeed, the
British Red Cross plays a vital role in helping
asylum seekers in destitution. But because of their
limited budget, they can only help for six to eight
weeks. There's no appeal. So if one is still destitute
after this time, tough luck.

Welsh Refugee Council receptionist
Are you an asylum seeker or a refugee?

Abdul

Me No Iglis Me Asylum

Welsh Refugee Council receptionist

Sorry we can't help you. Take this map and go to Migrant Help. *Half jokingly* We can only help refugees, not asylum seekers. Refugees are very important for us. We have to protect their rights and interests. You must go to Migrant Help.

Abdul

Walking out of the Refugee Council, he collapses. No, no, there's no need for such a dream.

He has been dreaming of the Ghakuya Café, were he last had coffee with his wife and daughter. He remembered that night when he had the vivid dream about Farsana. The café looked empty and deserted.

'Ghakuya Café'

The smell of coffee greets you
as you approach Ghakuya Café
the pitter patter of children's feet
big-bosomed women cladded and veiled

Here village gossip spreads
it was here we learned why
Abdi only has one testicle

At Ghakuya Café
I first saw my wife
it was here my uncle met Farsana

Rumours have it
all Eritrean athletes pass through Ghakuya Café
the place to be in the summer

The coffee is strong and extremely sweet
it is served with sweet bread
and popcorn

The women will then dance
forming a circle going round and round

something mysterious

My mother was certain the Ethiopians stole
coffee-making techniques from us

I miss Ghakuya
I miss my madina (my city)

'Abdul Dreams'

In the flowerbed of memory
Gharkuya Café has been my companion
I saw Gharkuya across horizons of lands beyond
here at Morgan Arcade I write of her
thin
haggard
abandoned
empty

if only she counted my wrinkles
many times I hit my head on stones
all but I can up and go
and I fly past many times
Gharkuya never said farewell

in this conclave
enslaved by these four walls
waiting on a Home Office postman
DPD UPS DHL
the waiting game torturous
kept alive by the flowerbeds of memory

my first kiss
first love bite
Gharkuya Café

never did we dream of exile
uncircumcised face of a dictator unknown

I am buried deep
as the king sips
my poetry memory drowns
in the flowerbed of exile

'Home Office'

My horror starts
when I enter the house

or when I see an envelope
with my name on it

the word 'Home office'

In the streets of Cardiff I roam
I am ashamed to laugh

I think I am mad
I must be

I laugh loud
I forget

I heard of a place called Gower
can I just up and go

Abdul has divided himself between Judge, Jury and
Prosecutor. All the maps he has collected are still
in his pocket, folded neatly.

Voices

Go to Migrant Help Map!
Go to Solicitor Map!
Go to Oasis Map!
Go to Trinity Centre Map!
Go to Refugee Council Map!

He is haggard, his face is vague, and he's not seen
a mirror in a while. His own body smell follows
him around. In the despair that has possessed him,
Abdul flies past his own house without realising.
He is flying, his eyes looking directly at the clock,
piercingly.

Abdul

Who said today was my day? How did it come to pass
that today was my last day on earth?

He remembers the last time he saw his mother, if

only he knew, if only someone had told him today
in a foreign land somewhere his name was written
among dead exiles. His daughter is now an orphan,
his wife will probably go and marry Hassan, his
nemesis.

If only I could have seen this day,
If only I had been warned,
I would have paid 30 pieces of gold more for my wife
and daughter to live behind concrete walls.

As he drifts into the clouds he disappears into the
bosom of his ancestors.

They saw the red moon
of cosmic concoction
doomsday whisperers
out with drums
singing choruses of end times

Why hast thou forsaken us

She journeyed from mental hibernation
an Old Testament Eremite
from beyond
foretelling an apocalypse

resurrected from the savannah
of the Bantu tribe
the lone survivor of a gas attack

dazed
a combined salutation of shadows
umbra penumbra
noise of trains clamouring
her head

though her eyes were opened
she was consumed
perpetual darkness
barking noises of dogs in heat

she was standing
yet falling
in her stutter she yelled

she was walking
yet floating

these are the walls
the guardsmen protected
the remnants of commonwealth soldiers

she fainted

Meanwhile an envelope arrives at Abdul's former Home Office accommodation address, sent from:

Removals Casework Co-ordination Team
Home Office – Immigration Enforcement
1st Floor, Vulcan House (Steel)
Sheffield
S3 8WA

To be continued...

Resources on Asylum Seeker Destitution

City of Sanctuary – resources, reports and links
cityofsanctuary.org/streams/destitution

Refugee Council UK – advice
tinyurl.com/refcouncildest

British Red Cross – 'Ending destitution': a call for changes to the system
tinyurl.com/redcrossdestitution

Faculty of Public Health – briefing on 'The health needs of asylum seekers'
tinyurl.com/fphdestitution

Oxfam – 'Coping with destitution' report
tinyurl.com/oxfamdestitution

Mind mental health charity – project on 'Improving mental health support for refugee communities'
tinyurl.com/minddestitution

Student Action for Refugees (STAR) – links
tinyurl.com/stardestitution

Home Office guide for asylum seekers
gov.uk/asylum-support

No Recourse to Public Funds Network – information shared by local authorities and partner organisations   nrpfnetwork.org.uk

Advice and Support in South Wales

Trinity Centre (Trinity Methodist Church) **Cardiff**
and **Cardiff Asylum Support Advocacy**
trinitycentre.wales

Space4U (Cardiff) www.space4ucardiff.co.uk

Oasis Centre (Cardiff) oasiscardiff.org

**Women Seeking Sanctuary Advocacy Group
(Cardiff)** wssagwales.wordpress.com

Cardiff Destitution Network
cardiffdestitutionnetwork.wordpress.com

Welsh Refugee Council welshrefugeecouncil.org

Displaced People in Action and **Wales Cities of
Sanctuary** dpia.org.uk

Swansea City of Sanctuary
swansea.cityofsanctuary.org

Swansea Bay Asylum Seekers Support Group
sbassg.wordpress.com

Unity in Diversity (Swansea)
uidswansea.wordpress.com

No Borders Wales
noborderswales.wordpress.com/refugee-destitution